CHRISTMAS

Program Builder No. 60

CHRISTMAS
Program Builder No. 60

Compiled by
Kim Messer

PO Box 419527
Kansas City, MO 64141

Questions? Please write or call:
Lillenas Publishing Company
Drama Resources
P. O. Box 419527
Kansas City, MO 64141
Phone: 816-931-1900 • Fax: 816-412-8390
E-mail: drama@lillenas.com
Web Site: www.lillenasdrama.com

Cover Design: J.R. Caines
Interior Design: Sharon Page

Contents

Recitations for Preschool

God's Own Promise

CHILD 1: Jesus in a manger lay
CHILD 2: Swaddled there upon the hay,
CHILD 3: Sleeping, keeping Christmas Day,
CHILD 4: God's own promise, heaven's "way."

Evelyn Mika

Prayer to Jesus

(A little girl comes out onstage and prays.)

Jesus, hear our prayer.
We know that You are near.
We thank You that You came.
We bless Your holy name.

K. R. Messer

Christmas Lives

Christmas lives
(CHILD *points toward heart)*
Inside of me,
And that's right where
It ought to be.

Robert Colbert

Thanks for Coming

(Use a precocious child for this piece and have some of the other children stand at the doors to hand out candy canes or another small gift as people exit.)

Thanks for coming to our play
I know you really want to stay
But now you have to go away
So have a really special day!

K. R. Messer

Hooray for Christmas Morning

BOYS: God above
Sent His love,
Gave His Son
To everyone.
ALL: This is Christmas morning.
GIRLS: Angels winging,
Wise men bringing,
Shepherds singing,
We've been won!
ALL: Hooray for Christmas morning!

Evelyn Mika

Sweet and Precious

Sweet and precious little man
Holding the world in Your hands.
We thank You for the gift You are.
You're the biggest, brightest Star.

Ray Ressem

Room for Thee

(To be recited at the manger)

CHILD 1: Gentle baby on the hay,
Come into my heart to stay.
CHILD 2: I have room enough for Thee.
You are welcome here with me.

Evelyn Mika

Christmas Box

(Wrap a box in festive paper that can be used for a special offering or collection at Christmas. The details of the collection can be given immediately after this short piece by a teen or adult. Have other children participate and serve as great examples by putting their gifts in during the announcement.)

CHILD 1: I love Jesus!
CHILD 2: I do too!
TOGETHER *(each pointing to themselves)*: He came for me.
(pointing to audience) He came for you.
CHILD 1: Merry Christmas!
CHILD 2: Christmas rocks!
TOGETHER: Please help us fill our Christmas box.

K. R. Messer

Christmas Love

God sent Jesus
From heaven above,
And this, my friends,
Is Christmas love.

Robert Colbert

I Wasn't Nice

I wasn't nice last week.
I hope it's not too late.
Christmas comes too quick
When you've made a big mistake.

But Grandpa told me that
I'm free from all my sins
If only I can let
The Christ child enter in.

Ray Ressem

Happy Birthday, Jesus

CHILD 1: Savior born
Christmas morn.
CHILD 2: Star bright,
Holy night.
CHILD 3: Angels praise,
Shepherds gaze.
ALL: Happy birthday, Jesus!
CHILD 4: Manger bed,
Halo head.
CHILD 5: Mary here,
Joseph near.
CHILD 6: Wise men three,
Gifts for Thee.
ALL: Happy birthday, Jesus!

Evelyn Mika

How He Came

(You can stage a short nativity scene during these verses and then sing a Christmas hymn with children's choir and congregation.)

On a donkey long ago
Mary and Joseph they did go.

No room for them in the city
Only a stable, what a pity!

Shepherds tending flocks at night
Angels in a heavenly light.

(Pointing to the manger) Baby Jesus,
there You are
Wise men followed that big star.

Welcome, Christmas baby boy,
Thank You for Your gift of joy!

K. R. Messer

Recitations for Ages 5 to 7

God's Gift of Love

Christmas is a time of joy.
Mary and Joseph's baby boy
Came to earth from heaven above.
Jesus Christ, God's gift of love.

Evelyn Mika

Welcome All

Welcome, Christmas friends.
It's time to celebrate.
You there in the back,
Sit down or you'll be late!

Welcome, Moms and Dads
And all that came today.
Thank you for your presence
It's time to start our play.

Ray Ressem

Welcome, Baby Jesus

(To be recited at the manger)

Baby Jesus, kind and true,
I would like to worship You
At Your manger kneel and pray,
Welcome You this Christmas Day.

Evelyn Mika

A Celebration

Christmas is a celebration.
Christ is born—
Mankind's salvation.

Robert Colbert

A Song for Him

(This is a piece to use before a short solo. "Away in a Manger" or another song can be used. Have the congregation join in on the second verse.)

I want to sing a song for Him,
My gift I want to bring.
I want to give all that I have
For Jesus, who's my King.

As you listen to my song,
A simple tune of love,
Think about how Jesus came
From heaven up above.

K. R. Messer

I'll Give My Heart

Gold and myrrh and frankincense
Carried from afar,
Delivered by three wise men
Following a star.

Gifts to Baby Jesus
I now want to bring.
"I'll give my heart; it's just the start,
My Savior and my King."

Evelyn Mika

Message for Hearts

(Two children come out in front of the kid's choir saying "Hi," "Hello," etc. They could also hold a sign that says, "Welcome."
Follow the piece immediately with a fun Christmas song.)

CHILD 1 *(to audience):* Did you come from far or near?
CHILD 2 *(to* CHILD 1*):* Makes no difference since they're here.
CHILD 1: It's our job to welcome them.
CHILD 2 *(pointing to someone):* Hey, who invited him?
CHILD 1: Teacher said to be nice.
CHILD 2: I know. She already told me twice.
CHILD 1 *(to audience):* Thank you for joining us today.
CHILD 2: Please listen to what we have to say.
CHILD 1: We have a message for your hearts.
CHILD 2: So settle in and we can start!

Ray Ressem

Proclaim His Birth

(Use this recitation with a slide or sign to prompt the audience to say the Bible verse, then follow with an energetic Christmas song led by the children.)

CHILD: God above sent His love
Born on Christmas Day.
May all on earth proclaim His birth
And with the angels say,
ALL: "Glory to God in the highest and on earth
peace, good will toward men." (Luke 2:14 [KJV])

Evelyn Mika

Our Wish for You

(As an option, a single speaker may be used)

GIRLS: There's a song in our hearts—
BOYS: It's a song of joy.
GIRLS: The Savior sent from heaven
BOYS: Was Mary's baby boy.
GIRLS: He lives in our hearts,
BOYS: And we're glad to say,
ALL: We wish you a Merry Christmas
And a Happy New Year's Day.

Margaret Primrose

Jesus in the Manger

CHILD 1: Mary and Joseph traveling far,
Darkness brightened by a star
Shining over where they are,
ALL: It's Jesus in the manger!
CHILD 2: Angels telling in the night,
Shepherds blinded by the light
Pointing to that precious sight,
ALL: It's Jesus in the manger!
CHILD 3: Wise men seeking, gifts they bring,
Baby worshiped, praise they sing
Honoring the newborn King.
ALL: It's Jesus in the manger!

Evelyn Mika

Today

(Break the children into small groups for this piece to help limit the lines they have to memorize, then have them all join in on the final verse.)

GROUP 1: Today you heard the story
Of how He came in glory.
A humble precious birth
To save us all on earth.
We hope you'll not forget.
We pray you'll cherish it.
GROUP 2: This tale we shared today
In our awesome play
Was put together for you
So you'd know what to do,
Give your life to Him
Then share the light with them. *(Pointing to the walls and doors of the church or outside)*
GROUP 3: Others deserve to see
The light He brought to me. *(Pointing to themselves)*
I'll celebrate this year
The One I hold so dear.
That's what it's about
I know without a doubt.
ALL: Merry Christmas, everyone!
Celebrate the Son!
Merry Christmas, one and all!
We hope you had a ball!

Ray Ressem

Recitations for Ages 8 to 10

Fill Our Hearts

Fill our hearts, dear Lord.
Fill them with the blessings of love.
Let us know the peace and joy
You brought from heaven above.
Robert Colbert

You Are Bigger

(An older boy or girl looking at the manger says or reads the following)

Little Baby in the hay,
You are bigger than You look.
You are big enough to save me.

Little Baby in the hay,
Your arms are longer than they look.
Your arms are wide enough to hold
the world.

Little Baby in the hay,
You are more beautiful than You
look now.
You are so beautiful that words
cannot really express how
much we love You.
Thank You for coming and thank
You for Your sacrifice. Amen.
K. R. Messer

A Bright Star

A star shining brightly in the dark
night
Gave wise men direction,
Set angels aflight
Proclaiming God's message
To shepherds that morn,
"Run to the manger, your Savior is
born!"
Evelyn Mika

The Miracle

Mary in a stable bare
Laid Jesus in a manger there,
Wrapped Him snugly in the hay
And so began their Christmas Day.

Wise men journeyed from afar
Guided by a brilliant star.
Shepherds ran to Bethlehem.
Angels told the news to them.

All just wanted to partake
Of God's sweet plan, for Jesus' sake.
The crowded inn, the stable fuss,
The miracle . . . God with us.
Evelyn Mika

When Jesus Came to Earth

(Use simple props to make this piece even more fun)

CHILD 1: No E-mail reservation
Had arrived at Bethlehem's inn.
But there was a hay-filled manger
For One who would save us from sin.

CHILD 2: There was no television
When Jesus came to earth,
But a multitude of angels
Announced the Savior's birth.

CHILD 3: No king nor priest was present,
But some shepherds heard them sing,
"Glory to God in the highest;
Praise God for the newborn King."

CHILD 4: The shepherds had no cell phones
To spread the news abroad,
But they were quick to share
A message that came from God.

CHILD 5: There were no maps nor billboards.
The wise men had no car,
But they were led to Jesus
By following a star.

CHILD 6: Though I've never seen Christ's birthplace,
I know the story's true.
I've read it in my Bible
And I believe that you have too.

Margaret Primrose

Brand-New Start

You've heard the Christmas story, so what will you do now?
Some of you are wondering; your question still is, "How?"
It's quite a tale of miracles, and we have doubting hearts.
Just remember that He came here to give you a brand-new start.

The baby in that manger grew up to save us all.
That same Savior listens every time you call.
Forgiven, and forgotten, your sins will fade away.
Ask Him without hesitation, He's ready for you today.

Ray Ressem

Plays & Monologues for All Ages

"On Earth Peace . . ."

(This may be done by an older student or teacher)

I was not there in days of old
As the announcement rang,
"God's glory in the highest,"
The host of angels sang.

I could not run with shepherds
To spread good news of joy,
"God's come to live among us;
He's Mary's baby boy."

I did not travel with them,
The wise men from afar,
Offering gifts to Jesus,
Directed by a star.

Still, this I know, God loved the
world
So much He gave His Son,
The "gift of life" if we believe
In what this Baby's done.

Yes, I believe these things are true;
They happened as God said,
And so because "today" is here
He's sending me instead.

(Children pass out candy kisses, hugs, or other small gift to those in attendance)

With love this little gift I give,
The song, good news I bring,
For you, a Christmas token—
For God, my offering.

Merry Christmas!

Evelyn Mika

Watch the Christmas Story

by Marilyn Millikan Holstein

Use a video to help the children portray the Christmas story. It is a fun learning process for all. This plan helps one to get the Christmas program ready early and eliminates last minute frustration and practice.

Early in November begin to record the video on Saturdays. Plan your presentation to tell the complete Christmas story beginning with the prophecy and ending with the holy family returning to Jerusalem.

If you have a large group of children, divide them into three groups for the taping with just the main characters present each time. In a small group, children may be used over and over. Have several crowd scenes to assure using all the children.

Costumes should be the usual biblical dress. Props will consist of gifts for the wise men, crooks and sticks for the shepherds, bundles for pilgrims, home furnishings for the house of Mary and Joseph, and live or fake animals.

Settings can be arranged in three areas: the church, a farm or park, and at nighttime outdoors. Take as many pictures as you can and use as many as possible. Do not expect professional performance from your actors. Their innocent ways, expressions, and actions will add human interest.

For the farm setting, try to make arrangements for a farm with live animals, a rugged manger, and open fields where there are no modern buildings to clutter the landscape.

Photo scenes might include the following:

1. Outdoors depicting a street with a Roman soldier giving the taxation proclamation to the people
2. Mary on donkey with Joseph walking
3. Manger scene, in the stable
4. Manger scene with Mary and Joseph
5. Manger scene with Mary, Joseph, and baby
6. The shepherds around a campfire
7. Angels appearing to shepherds
8. Shepherds show fear
9. Shepherds leave to go to Bethlehem
10. The shepherds with the holy family in Bethlehem
11. The shepherds depart to return to the fields
12. The wise men following the star
13. The wise men seeing the star over the stable

14. The holy family with the wise men
15. The wise men leaving the stable
16. Modern children kneeling before the manager in an attitude of prayer and worship
17. Herod with advisors
18. Herod, advisors, and wise men
19. Mary, Joseph, and baby with Simeon
20. Mary, Joseph, and baby with Anna
21. Crowd scenes using other children

Scripture suggestions for each video picture:

1. Luke 2:1, 3
2. Luke 2:4, 5
3. Luke 2:7
4. Matthew 1:21
5. Matthew 1:23
6. Luke 2:8
7. Luke 2:9
8. Luke 2:10-12
9. Luke 2:19
10. Luke 2:15, 16
11. Luke 2:17, 18
12. Matthew 2:1, 2
13. Matthew 2:8, 9
14. Matthew 2:10, 11
15. Matthew 2:12
16. Luke 2:14
17. Matthew 2:3
18. Matthew 2:4, 5
19. Luke 2:25-28
20. Luke 2:36, 37

Production Notes

About three weeks before the program, arrange your pictures in order along with the scriptures. Assign a scripture to each child or several children. If only a small group, let each child have more than one scripture. Ask the children to memorize their scripture if possible and have the teachers drill them.

Type out a draft listing the pictures, the corresponding scriptures, and the child's name beside the slide number. This is to guide the prompters. Use a handheld microphone for the children to use for the scriptures. The microphone can be passed from one to another. The various voices with different inflections and sounds adds to the effect.

Ask the pianist or organist to use soft music as a background.

This will be one of the best programs you have had and all will be touched by the sacredness.

Voices of Christmas

by Beth Westcott

Cast:

NARRATOR
MARY
JOSEPH
SHEPHERD
WISE MAN
SIMEON
ANNA

Prelude

Pastoral Prayer

Scripture: But when the time had come, God sent his Son, born of a woman, born under law, to redeem those under law, that we might receive the full rights of sons. Because you are sons, God sent the Spirit of his Son into our hearts, the Spirit who calls out, "Abba, Father." (Gal. 4:4-6)

Congregational Song: "O Come, All Ye Faithful"

MARY: It happened so suddenly. I didn't expect it. Every woman in Israel hoped she would be the one—the Chosen One, the Blessed One. But I didn't really expect it would be me. The great Jehovah uses the simple and foolish to confound the great and wise.

I looked up and there he was—Gabriel. He was brilliant and pure, a holy angel, sent to me, a poor peasant girl. Yes, my genealogical chart said that I was a descendant of Kind David. Still, I could only fall down trembling. Surely it was God's judgment. But, no, Gabriel spoke to me gently, "Fear not, Mary. You have found favor with God."

Favor with God? Me? What did Gabriel mean?

"God has chosen you to be the mother of a special Child. This Child will be the Son of God himself."

"How can this be?" I asked. "I am not married." I would never consider becoming pregnant before being married. It would dishonor God. And it would dishonor my betrothed, Joseph.

"Don't worry, Mary. The Holy Spirit will make it possible. God will be the Father of this Child."

What could I do? If God willed it to be so, then so be it.

"I am God's handmaiden," I said. "Let God use me however He will."

To be the mother of the Christ, the Savior—God's Son. I had much to think about. What an honor! What a dilemma! I could not understand how it was to be, but my heart and soul were lifted up in praise to Jehovah.

Scripture: And Mary said: My soul glorifies the Lord and my spirit rejoices in God my Savior, for he has been mindful of the humble state of his servant. From now on all generations will call me blessed, for the Mighty One has done great things for me—holy is his name. His mercy extends to those who fear him, from generation to generation. He has performed mighty deeds with his arm; he has scattered those who are proud in their inmost thoughts. He has brought down rulers from their thrones but has lifted up the humble. He has filled the hungry with good things but has sent the rich away empty. He has helped his servant Israel, remembering to be merciful to Abraham and his descendants forever, even as he said to our fathers. (Luke 1:46-55)

NARRATOR: How about you? Are you willing to lay your life on the line for God? Do you think it was easy for Mary? How could she explain this pregnancy? How could she face her relatives and neighbors and tell them her child would be the Messiah. I'm sure they laughed in her face. And Joseph, her betrothed, wouldn't he feel betrayed? Mary didn't understand it all, nor could she see what lay ahead. But she was willing to take a step—no, a leap of faith in order to yield herself to God's will. I wonder if she knew by heart the verses in Proverbs, "Trust in the LORD with all your heart, and lean not on your own understanding: In all your ways acknowledge him, and he will make your paths straight." (Prov. 3:5-6)

Congregational Song: "What Child Is This?"

JOSEPH: What was I to do? My fiancé was with child. What was I to think but that she was being unfaithful to me? Unbelievable to think that of a sweet, gentle woman like Mary. I did not want to see her die. But the law was clear—adultery was punishable by stoning. What was I to do? My reputation was on the line too. I decided to divorce her privately to spare her embarrassment.

Then Gabriel appeared to me in a dream. He told me that Mary's child was also God's Child. He was to be the Savior of the world—Immanuel—God with us. God told me I should go ahead and marry her. She had not been unfaithful at all! God had chosen Mary and me to look after His Son while He was growing up as a human being. Parents of the Son of God—awesome!

Mary became my wife and I brought her to my home. I did not know all that would happen, but I obeyed God.

NARRATOR: Think how the tongues wagged when Joseph married Mary and she was already expecting a child. I wonder how many people knew. Nazareth was not a large city, and you know how gossip travels. I wonder if Joseph's carpentry business suffered for a while. Or did Mary and Joseph have reputations that would put aside the whispers of immorality? Was Joseph burdened with a tremendous sense of responsibility to be the earthly father of the Son of God? Did he sometimes wonder if he had made the right choice? Did he sometimes wonder if he would succeed as a father?

Congregational Song: "Ring the Bells"

Special: "O Holy Night"

SHEPHERD: Wow! What an experience! I couldn't believe it! There we were, watching the sheep that night. Suddenly there was a brilliant, blinding light! We were so afraid we couldn't even stand up. Our legs were like jelly and our knees knocked together. But that angel said, "Don't be afraid. I have great, joyful news to tell you. The Savior was born in Bethlehem tonight. Go and see Him. You'll find Him swaddled in cloths, lying in a manger." And then the other angels came and praised God.

The Savior—our expected Messiah—in a smelly manger in a smelly stable? What was God thinking? Well, we decided to go. The sheep were in the fold for the night. One of us had to stay behind to protect them, and I was glad it wasn't me! What an experience! To see the Messiah firsthand! His mother and father looked so . . . so common. And He was just a wee baby, sweet, tender, and helpless. We lowly shepherds saw Him and worshiped Him there. We didn't keep it quiet, though. We told everyone we met—the Messiah had come!

Special: "While by Our Sheep"

NARRATOR: Did you ever wonder why Jesus was born in a stable rather than a palace? Would the shepherds have been welcome in a palace? Did you ever wonder why He came as a baby rather than a conquering hero? Most people respond tenderly to a baby, but would fear a conqueror. Jesus will one day come again as a conquering King, but for now He was approachable and accessible. He is still that way. "But as many as received Him, to them gave He the power to become the sons of God . . ."

The shepherds couldn't keep quiet. Can you?

Congregational Song: "Go Tell It on the Mountain"

WISE MAN: That brilliant star must mean something!

Long ago, Jewish captives told us about a star that would appear to announce the birth of a King. If the king were that important, we certainly must see Him and honor Him!

It was a long, arduous journey to Jerusalem and to Bethlehem. We traveled in a large caravan because of highwaymen who would attack, kill, and rob unsuspecting travelers. There was safety in numbers. It was worth it all, to bow down before the Child and present to Him our gifts of gold, frankincense, and myrrh. These were gifts befitting the King, the pure Son of God, and the Savior of mankind.

Praise be to the Lord God Jehovah for His unspeakable gift!

Special: "We Three Kings," (verses 1 and 4)

NARRATOR: How much are you willing to give to know Jesus? The wise men traveled a long way to honor Him, and they brought Him expensive gifts. These pagan scholars recognized His importance. Do you?

Congregational Song: "Thou Didst Leave Thy Throne"

SIMEON: I have seen God's salvation for Israel. I held Him in these old, trembling arms. Praise God! I knew Him as soon as I saw Him—God's Spirit led me to the Temple that day, at that moment. A young Jewish couple entered with a baby, their firstborn son, to present Him to Jehovah as commanded in the Law. My heart leaped within my breast. I knew Him! I have seen God's salvation for Israel!

But, as I warned the mother, His way would not be easy, His life would not be trouble free. He had a special purpose to fulfill—God's purpose!

Thank You, Lord, for fulfilling Your promise to me. Thank You for letting me see this Child, who will one day be a light to the Gentiles and salvation for my people. Now I will depart from this life in peace.

ANNA: I knew the minute I saw Him! Here He was, the One I had waited so long to see! And I, Anna, an old, old woman, held the Messiah in my arms. I never had children of my own. My husband died early in our marriage. But now, God has rewarded my faithfulness to Him after all these years. Oh, the precious, precious Baby. How sweet and tender, like so many babies.

But He is not just like other babies. He is God's Promised One, the One to redeem Israel. How long we have waited for God's redemption. Now God has fulfilled His promise at this time, for His purposes. Now

I may go to my grave rejoicing and with thankfulness in my heart to Jehovah.

Congregational Song: "Joy to the World"

NARRATOR: Are you celebrating this Christmas with thankfulness in your heart? Have you received His gift of salvation through Jesus Christ? "For God so loved the world that he gave his only begotten Son, that whosoever believeth in him should not perish, but have everlasting life." (John 3:16 [KJV]) At Christmas we celebrate the birth of a baby, God's only begotten Son. However, Jesus did not remain a baby. If we worship only the Baby in a manger, we are not truly worshiping God. Jesus grew up to manhood, and after three years of teaching, healing, and helping, He was arrested, tried, and hung on the cross. He did not deserve the punishment. The charges against Him were trumped up, false, misleading. His trial was held illegally. He did not suffer for His own sin, for He was the sinless Son of God. He suffered and died for the sins of the whole world, including yours and mine. "He was wounded for our transgressions, he was bruised for our iniquities: . . . and with his stripes we are healed. (Isa. 53:5 [KJV]) Let us rejoice in God's gift of love—His Son. Let us also rejoice in the fulfillment of His promise through the ages to send a Savior.

Congregational Song: "Angels We Have Heard on High"

Candlelight Service Music: "Silent Night"

Little Star

A Christmas Play for the Young at Heart

by Joyce Warrall, adapted by Susan Wood

Theme: Christmas

Cast:

Narrator
Little Star
Twinkle
Star 1
Star 2
Star 3
Great Creator—Offstage voice
Star Puppets—Three to eight persons
Mary
Joseph
Shepherds—Three to five persons
Wise Men—Three persons
Song Leader
(Note: Twinkle, the Stars, Great Creator, and the puppeteers can double as the living nativity characters.)

Props:

5 ladders
Stool
Large storybook
5 "Star" T-shirts
Star Puppets (simple large gold stars on sticks work well)
Clump of gold ribbons
Manger
Doll (serves as the baby Jesus)
3 gifts for wise men

Scene: The stable containing the manger is CS hidden under cloth. On either side of the stable, there are partitions covered in more cloth. On the right side of the stable, three ladders are set behind the partitions while one ladder is directly behind the stable, and the last ladder is SL. The stool and the large storybook for the Narrator are far SL in front of the partitions.

(As the lights come up, NARRATOR *is seated on the stool with the storybook in hand.)*

NARRATOR *(reading):* Once upon a time, in fact, it was the very beginning of time, God—the Great Creator—made the stars. (LITTLE STAR, TWINKLE, *and* STARS 1, 2, *and* 3, *each wearing a star T-shirt, appear from different sides of the* STAR PUPPETS *and spread out evenly behind the partitions.)* Then the Great Creator told the stars . . .

GREAT CREATOR: I have a special place for each of you to shine, and a special job for each of you to do. But you will have to wait until I'm finished making the rest of the universe before you can be placed in the sky.

*(*STARS 1, 2, *and* 3, TWINKLE, *and* LITTLE STAR *line up in that order from left to right.)*

NARRATOR: They waited. All of them were so excited thinking about where in the heavens they would be placed. They even whispered among themselves about the special jobs they might do.

(All STARS *make whispering noises)*

NARRATOR: They all whispered quietly, except Little Star. (LITTLE STAR *is fidgeting.)* She was so excited that she just couldn't stay quiet.

LITTLE STAR *(loudly):* Just think! I'm going to have a place to shine for the Great Creator!

STAR 1 *(very disapprovingly):* Quiet, you!

STAR 2 *(scolding):* Not so loud!

STAR 3 *(haughtily):* Please!

LITTLE STAR *(lowering voice):* Ah, I'm sorry. I can't help it. *(Her voice continues to rise as she speaks.)* I'm just so excited! It's just hard to be quiet!

STARS 1, 2, 3: Shhhh!

LITTLE STAR *(softly but excitedly to* TWINKLE*):* Just think, Twinkle, you and me, shining for the Great Creator!

TWINKLE *(also excited, but quietly):* I know! I know!

LITTLE STAR *(loudly):* That's a really big job!

STAR 1: Shhhh!

STAR 2: That's enough!

STAR 3: Quiet!

NARRATOR: Finally, the waiting was over.

(As the following lines are read, STARS 1, 2, *and* 3, *and* TWINKLE *exit.* STARS 1, 2, *and* 3 *reappear atop the three ladders SR and* TWINKLE *atop the ladder SL. The* STAR PUPPETS *settle down into a place.)*

NARRATOR: One by one, the Great Creator took each of the stars and showed them exactly where and how they were to shine for Him. *(*LITTLE STAR *moves to CS and waits anxiously.)* At last He came to Little Star. Thoughtfully, He looked down at the excited little one.

GREAT CREATOR: Do you really want to shine for me, Little Star?

LITTLE STAR *(looking up)*: Yes, Sir! I want to shine for You so much! Anywhere! Anytime!

GREAT CREATOR: Good, because I have a very special place for you and a very important job. Only, you will have to wait because now is not the right time.

NARRATOR: And with that, the Great Creator was gone. *(Pause)* Little Star was confused. She didn't know what to do. She looked into the heavens where all of the other stars were shining and felt very much alone. *(*LITTLE STAR *sits in the fetal position CS.)*

STAR 1 *(from atop her ladder)*: Did you hear what happened to Little Star?

*(*STAR PUPPETS *react excitedly to the gossip while* LITTLE STAR *listens with apprehension.)*

STAR 2, 3: No, do tell!

STAR 1: She wasn't placed!

STAR 2: Wasn't *placed*? But how could that be? Everyone else was.

STAR 3: Far be it from me to say that the Great Creator could ever make a mistake, but do you remember who was so noisy when we were waiting in line for our job assignments?

STAR 1: Oh yes. That's right.

STAR 2: Just terrible.

NARRATOR: On and on the other stars talked until Little Star became very upset and frightened. She fled to her friend Twinkle.

LITTLE STAR *(rushing to stand near* TWINKLE*)*: What am I going to do, Twink? Maybe the Great Creator did make a mistake when He made me. Maybe there isn't a special job after all . . . maybe . . . *(pause with horror)* maybe I'm a mistake . . .

TWINKLE: Now, just hold on, Little Star. You know the Great Creator doesn't make mistakes.

LITTLE STAR: But what am I going to do?

TWINKLE: Hmm . . . let me think . . . suppose you were to grow a big star beam so everyone would notice you.

LITTLE STAR *(smiling):* A star beam! I can do that! What a wonderful idea! A star beam! If I make it big enough, everyone will notice me. Maybe even the Great Creator will see it and then give me a place to shine for Him. Thanks, Twinkle! I've got to get busy on my star beam. *(Exits SL)*

NARRATOR: She went right to work and soon Little Star had a beautiful star beam. *(*LITTLE STAR *reenters with a clump of gold ribbons hanging from one of the star points on her T-shirt or from one of her wrists while the other* STARS *nod and smile)* All of the other stars watched with approving interest.

*(*STAR PUPPETS *also react with excitement and* LITTLE STAR *dances around the stage fluttering her star beam.)*

STAR 1: Hmmm, perhaps she'll amount to something after all.

STAR 2: Perhaps.

STAR 3: Could be.

NARRATOR: Little Star's star beam was indeed one of the most beautiful in all of the heavens, and just as she had wanted, it caught the eye of the Great Creator.

GREAT CREATOR: What do we have here, little one?

LITTLE STAR *(proudly displaying the star beam):* Sir, I grew this star beam so I can be good enough to shine for You.

GREAT CREATOR: That star beam is for Me?

LITTLE STAR: Oh, yes, Sir, it sure is! And I'll shine anyplace for You. Please, give me a chance.

GREAT CREATOR: If it is for Me, and I can use it exactly the way I want . . .

LITTLE STAR: Yes, it's Yours!

GREAT CREATOR: Then, may I break it off?

LITTLE STAR *(upset):* Break it off! Why would You want to break it off? It's for You so I can shine for You! I did it for You! *(Pause as she struggles with her decision)* I suppose You can break it off, if You *really* want to.

GREAT CREATOR: Thank you, precious one. You see, I can't use you the way I planned with this star beam in the way.

(LITTLE STAR *exits SL and removes the clump of gold ribbons)*

NARRATOR: With enormous care and infinite love, the Great Creator took Little Star in His hands and carefully broke off the star beam. He put the broken little one inside His cloak right next to His heart and then went about His work. Little Star could still hear the other stars talking.

STAR 1: Did you hear what happened to Little Star?

STARS 2, 3: No, do tell.

NARRATOR: But as time went by, they didn't matter anymore.

(TWINKLE, STARS 1, 2, *and* 3, *and the* STAR PUPPETS *all drop out of sight.)*

NARRATOR: Little Star was learning to listen to another voice as she lived day by day close to the Great Creator's heart. And after a very long time, the Great Creator called softly to Little Star.

GREAT CREATOR: Now, little one, now is the time for you to shine for Me! Follow My finger across the sky and I will point to your place in the heavens.

NARRATOR: Joy filled Little Star's heart. There really was a special job after all. Little Star started to follow the hand of the Great Creator until she noticed the direction it was going. Down, down, down . . . far below all of the other stars. So very far down near the earth.

GREAT CREATOR: Stop! Stop here, little one, and shine for Me!

(LITTLE STAR *appears on the ladder CS just above the hidden stable.)*

NARRATOR: As Little Star watched, people approached.

(MARY *and* JOSEPH *enter SR.* JOSEPH *pulls away the cloth from the stable to reveal the manger.* MARY *and* JOSEPH *settle in with the doll [baby] in* MARY'S *arms.)*

NARRATOR *(with tremendous awe):* Little Star could hardly believe what she was seeing. She was shining to announce the birth of the Great Creator's Son. God's only Son—Jesus! She had been made for this!

(Throughout the rest of the play, a spotlight will shine on LITTLE STAR *and grow slowly larger until the end.)*

NARRATOR: Little Star watched as Mary, Joseph, and Baby Jesus settled down in the simple stable. They stayed there because there was no room for them in the inn.

(SONG LEADER *leads congregation in "Away in the Manger.")*

NARRATOR: Not far away, in another part of the sky, Little Star saw angels appear. They were telling a group of shepherds that Jesus, God's only Son, had been born. The angels told the shepherds that they would find the baby wrapped in cloth and lying in a manger. The shepherds couldn't get to the stable fast enough to see the miracle.

(SHEPHERDS *enter from the audience and make their way to the stage to gather around the manger with* MARY *and* JOSEPH.)

(SONG LEADER *leads congregation in "Hark the Herald Angels Sing"*)

NARRATOR: Then Little Star saw wise men from distant lands making their way toward her. They kept pointing up at her and watching her. She realized they were following her. They were using her light to find Jesus.

(WISE MEN *enter from the audience carrying gifts and make their way to the stage to join the group at the manger. By now, the spotlight on* LITTLE STAR *should be at its fullest.*)

(SONG LEADER *leads congregation in "O Come, All Ye Faithful"*)

NARRATOR: As Little Star looked down and saw Baby Jesus, her heart was filled with joy. Slowly, without her even knowing it, she had grown from just a little star into the brightest and most beautiful star in all of the heavens. *(Pause)* And she didn't even know it.

(SONG LEADER *leads congregation in "Joy to the World"*)

(*A pastor comes forward to lead in a closing prayer as the living nativity and* LITTLE STAR *remain in place.*)

No Room at the Inn

by Susan A. Tough

Scripture References: Isaiah 7:14; Micah 5:2; Matthew 1:18-25; Luke 1:26-38, 2:1-20 (NIV)

Cast:

MOSHE—Middle-aged male innkeeper of Jewish descent
DINA—Innkeeper's wife, also Jewish

Scene:

It's the night of Christ's birth; Jewish innkeepers Dina and Moshe have just turned away Mary and Joseph from a room at their inn, giving them a place in the stables instead. After all, they are holding a room for their regular high-paying guest, Romulus, a Roman official. Dina is remorseful, while her husband Moshe is happy to be rid of the young couple. Can angels or shepherds or his nagging wife convince this once devout Jew that this baby is really the Messiah?

Setting:

Scene opens inside a typical Middle-Eastern inn in Bethlehem on the night of Jesus' birth. The room contains a window made of wood slats or with shutters and a door. There's a cedar chest serving as a table, a couple of stools, and a throw rug on the floor. On the table, there's a hard round loaf of bread, a water jug, some white cloths, some salt, and an oil lamp. Another oil lamp is burning near the window to indicate it is evening.

Scene 1

*(*DINA *is gazing out the window as the scene opens. She and* MOSHE *are involved in an argument.)*

MOSHE: Dina, will you come away from there and see to our guests? I don't know what's come over you. You've been gazing out that window for days now. You haven't gone to the market, my clothes are not getting mended *(picks up a rock hard loaf of bread and bangs it on the table)* and this bread is as stale as Rabbi's last teaching.

DINA *(staring out at the night sky):* It's that strange light out there in the sky. I can't stop looking at it . . . wondering what it could mean. It looks like . . . I don't know. I've never seen anything like it. *(Turning away from the window)* I think it was wrong to send that young couple away without giving them a room. That young girl was ready to deliver her baby.

MOSHE: Don't be ridiculous. We turn away visitors every day. We don't have space for everyone—and with all these people coming to town to register for the census, what did they expect?

DINA: I know . . . Did you see the look on the woman's face when we refused them? Her cloak was threadbare—hardly thick enough to shield her from the cold wind. Her fingers were like ice. She tried to press a few coins into my hand to pay for a room. It must have been all they had. And him—you could see the exhaustion in his eyes. Oh Moshe, we should have made room for them.

MOSHE: We did make room—down in the stables. That's more than anyone else in this town did for them. It'll be warm enough for them with the animals. And there's plenty of fresh hay to use as a bed.

DINA: You're a hard man. *(Picks up the bread)* Even harder than this stale loaf of bread. At least it has a soft center. You're as hard as the rocks that line our streets. What's happened to you?

MOSHE: It's business, that's all. Now, quit your complaining and get back to work. You know as well as I do we have no room for them.

DINA: We would have a room if you weren't holding it for that Roman centurion.

MOSHE: Don't you start in about Romulus again. If it weren't for him, you and I would be out on the streets and maybe even dead by now. He provides protection for us and for the business. Plus, he has promised to put in a good word for me with Caesar. It could mean a government position for me. We could finally get out of Bethlehem and move to the big city where we really belong—maybe even Jerusalem. I'd sell this hovel and buy us a real house with a courtyard and fountains and our own servants. We could really start to live. With Romulus' help, we could . . .

DINA *(cutting him off)*: Romulus this and Romulus that! You'd think the man walked on water! There are much more important things in life—like that young couple out in the stable. *(She picks up the water jug, cloths, salt, and lamp and heads for the door.)*

MOSHE: Where do you think you're going? Who's going to prepare for Romulus' arrival? You could have at least laid out some cheese and olives for him and baked some fresh bread. An honored guest is arriving and we have nothing to set before him.

DINA: Just keep filling his mug with wine and flattering him. That's all he cares about anyway. I'm going to do what's right in the Lord's sight and help that girl with the birth. Her time is near. *(Exits)*

MOSHE *(calling out the door):* Dina, come back here. I won't have you midwifing for a peasant. Do you hear me? What will Romulus think if he sees you out there in the stable like a common slave? You are the mistress of this house . . . *(turns back toward the table)*

Oh, what's the use? She'll never understand me—after all I've done for her too. And she has to mention the Lord to me. Where was He when the Romans took over our land? I had no choice but to make peace with them. *(Wanders to the window and stares out)* She was right about one thing though; there is a strange light out there. What could it mean?

I better get back to work. The hour is late. *(Hesitates and turns back to the window, looking up)* Lord, how could You forget us? You promised to send us a messiah—a deliverer. How could You let us fall into the hands of the Romans? *(Angry now)* Where is this great king You promised us? Do You think I like playing the fool in front of Romulus?

Those peasants out there are nothing. Romulus has the power to change my life.

(Scene fades out to music or just a pause to show time passage.)

Scene 2

(Lights up)

DINA *(rushing in out of breath):* Oh Moshe! The baby is beautiful! His face glows. It's the strangest thing. I couldn't tell if it was coming from the light in the sky or from Him.

MOSHE *(backing away):* Dina, you smell like the goats. Now sit down and come to your senses. I don't want Romulus to arrive and think I'm married to a madwoman.

DINA: I've no wish to argue with you at a time like this. I've seen Him, Moshe. *(Eyes glaze over)* I've seen Him with my own eyes.

MOSHE *(perplexed):* Seen who? You're not making any sense.

DINA: The Messiah. He's here!

MOSHE: Here? *(Looking around)* Where?

DINA: No! Out there—in the stable. The baby . . . don't you see. He's the one we've been waiting for. The couple, Joseph and Mary, they told me the whole story. In between her pains, Mary told me that an angel from the Lord appeared to her and told her she was going to have a son. She said it was a miracle because she wasn't married and had never been with a man.

MOSHE: Those two weren't married? The baby's illegitimate. I won't stand for it! *(Starts toward the door)* I won't have those kind of people in my place of business.

DINA: Moshe, wait! You have to hear the rest of the story—Joseph's part. Joseph felt the same way you did at first—that the child was illegitimate. He was going to call off their engagement then and there. But an angel appeared to him too. The angel told him the child she was carrying was from the Holy Spirit. They were to call Him Jesus because He would save His people from their sins. So the next morning, Joseph took Mary as his wife.

MOSHE *(shaking his head):* Dina, I'm beginning to think you're touched in the head. You can't tell me you believe this crazy story? All this talk of angels. They don't even exist.

DINA: You used to believe that angels existed. You used to believe everything the Scriptures said. What's happened to you? *(Pause)* Come with me, Moshe. Come and meet Jesus, our long-awaited Messiah.

MOSHE: I'm staying right here to meet my long-awaited guest, Romulus.

DINA: He's not here? You could still give his room to Joseph and Mary.

MOSHE: Oh, that would go over well! "Uh, Romulus, I'm sorry there's no room at the inn tonight . . . so you'll be sleeping in the barn with the goats!" No, thank you. I have no intention of jeopardizing our future.

DINA: Why couldn't he stay in the stables? There's plenty of fresh hay out there, isn't that what you said?

MOSHE: Don't ask me about that room again or I'll have those peasants thrown out of the stable as well!

DINA: May the Lord forgive you. *(Stomps out)*

MOSHE *(to himself):* Messiah indeed! As if I'm to believe our King and Redeemer is the son of peasants. If the real Messiah were here, we'd never be in the hands of Caesar. My hopes for the Messiah coming in my lifetime died with my father. He was always dreaming that the Scriptures were true and that the Messiah would come to save him. Little good it did. He's dead now—along with everyone else who opposed Rome. Well, I refuse to end up on the losing side like him! *(Paces around furiously)* Romulus, where are you?

(Fade out to song or lights down to indicate passage of time.)

Scene 3

(Lights up. DINA *rushes back in, beaming.)*

MOSHE *(peering out the window):* What's all that commotion outside? All that braying of donkeys and bleating of sheep. Who are all those people out by the stables?

DINA: It's the shepherds. They've come in from the fields to see Jesus.

MOSHE: What! So now He has visitors calling on Him as if He were some kind of royalty? And just how did these shepherds find out He was here?

DINA: Uh . . . well . . .

MOSHE *(raising his hand to silence her):* Don't tell me. Let me guess. An angel told them.

DINA *(sheepishly):* Well . . . yes . . . now that you mention it. One angel came and told them that a Savior had been born and that they would find Him in a manger here in Bethlehem. Then a whole group of angels appeared and lit up the sky where the shepherds were tending their flocks. Of course, the shepherds came at once to see the baby.

MOSHE: Well, I hope they don't intend to stay long. Romulus is not used to such low-class people. I don't want the inn overtaken with peasants and low-life shepherds.

DINA: And their flocks. Don't forget their flocks.

MOSHE: Why is this happening to me? Just when things were starting to look up.

DINA: There's still time to do right and give Joseph and Mary a room. It doesn't even look like Romulus is coming.

MOSHE: I will not have those peasants in the room I have saved for my honored guest and besides, he's already here.

DINA: I give up. I can see that just as there's no room in this inn for those peasants, there's no room in your heart for the Messiah of our people!

MOSHE: You are talking nonsense! I told you I do not believe He's the Messiah. Why should I believe the word of peasants and shepherds?

DINA: Then believe God's words. You told me the Messiah's birth was foretold in the Scriptures hundreds of years ago. Something about "they will call him Immanuel" which means God with us. Oh Moshe, I don't know the Scriptures like you do. You, of all people, should remember.

MOSHE: I don't know what you're talking about. I don't remember anything about that—nor do I care to.

DINA: You have to remember something. You've heard the Scriptures recited over and over again since you were a young boy. Your father was the keeper of the scrolls for the synagogue and you spent all those years helping him.

MOSHE: My father is dead and so is my hope in a Messiah! *(Turning away from her)* Now leave me alone.

DINA *(sadly):* If your father were here, he'd wonder what happened to his son just like I'm wondering what happened to my husband. *(Exits)*

MOSHE *(pacing around restlessly):* Leave it to her to bring up my father at a time like this. First, it's the Lord and now it's my father. Yes, Father, if you were here, I'm sure you'd be the first one to pay your respects to King Jesus, second in line only to my dreamer of a wife. How I wish I had your faith. *(Pause)*

"Immanuel—God with us."

"The virgin will be with child and will give birth to a son, and will call him, Immanuel."

(Thinking) Could it really be true . . .? Here in Bethlehem? *(Paces around more and then the light dawns)* Bethlehem? Yes! "But you Bethlehem Ephrathah, out of you will come for me, one who will be ruler over Israel . . ."

My Lord, this is the Messiah that You promised!

(Hurries over and opens the cedar chest and pulls out a beautiful prayer shawl.)

Father, this was your most precious possession. *(Puts it around his shoulders and admires it, feeling the tassels.)* I had hoped to pass it down to my own son, but now I see it was meant for someone else.

(Takes off the shawl and folds it up neatly)

It's going to be a cold night and that baby outside is going to need a blanket.

(Takes the shawl and heads out the door. Lights fade.)